WITH THE PEOPLE

An Introduction to an Idea

David Mathews

A Cousins Research Group Report

Kettering Foundation Press

Dear Reader,

As I write this, the world is dealing with the deadly coronavirus pandemic. It not only endangers our health, it threatens us with feelings of hopelessness, of being unable to control what is happening. We are most vulnerable to this despair when we are alone. The antidote is the strength that comes from joining with others to shape *B.R.* our future, in whatever way we can. This report is about what can be accomplished by working *with* one another and *with* the institutions that we created to serve us. We are already seeing some of that happening, beginning in our communities. However, there will be obstacles that stand in the way, and they will loom larger once the crisis fades a bit. There is no vaccine that will prevent future crises or the despair they bring with them. But where there is resilience, it will be found in us, The People.

This is an overview of a longer and more complete book titled, *With: Another Way of Thinking about the Relationship between People and Governing Institutions*. It explores, in more detail, the possibility of a better relationship between the American people and their governing institutions. The unabridged version, which took years to complete, is in debt to so many researchers and editors that a complete acknowledgment would be about as long as the book itself. However, their names and contributions are etched in stone in the Kettering Foundation archives.

While that cast of thousands certainly contributed to this abridged overview, it wouldn't have existed without Laura Carlson, its chief editor; Lisa Boone-Berry, copy editor; and Sherri Goudy, who checked facts and located sources. I write by hand, and that produced reams of confusion. I owe an unpayable debt of appreciation to our administrative assistant, Kathy Heil, who brought order out of chaos. This group truly worked *with* one another.

David Mathews
April 20, 2020

Many Americans have been troubled by our political system for some time. They live in all parts of the country and have different reasons for being concerned. Some fear that America itself is in decline because of an erosion of our core values and problems in the way our political system works—or doesn't work.[1] Others are troubled by a growing economic divide, along with racial and other forms of injustice.[2] People usually blame politicians for what they don't like, while political leaders often point fingers at what they see as an irresponsible public. Whatever the reasons, many people have lost confidence in our major governing institutions, and their discontent has increased over time.[3]

We need all of our governing institutions working effectively to deal with crises like the coronavirus pandemic. They can't do that without being reinforced by the work citizens do.

What Are "Governing" Institutions? I think of governing, at its most basic, as the organization of collective efforts for collective well-being. The institutions that do the governing have authority that is granted by citizens and legally conferred or based on their expertise. The governing system is made up of institutions that range from the local to the national level. They are the legislative, executive, and judicial branches of government. I include nongovernmental bodies like schools, foundations, and civic organizations as well. No matter what form they take, many of these authoritative institutions suffer from declining public confidence and support.*

---

* In a report to Kettering, *America: Where to from Here?* (October 2017), Rich Harwood, drawing on his experience with institutions that have lost public trust (including local ones like schools), located one source of the alienation in people's perception that institutions pursue their own agendas and not those of the citizenry. Harwood thinks this problem is related to the kind of professionalism that disposes institutional staffs to impose their own solutions on people and their communities. This creates a relationship with the public that robs citizens of their ability to control or at least shape their future.

THE CHALLENGES FACING OUR DEMOCRACY

Losing Trust

The fall in confidence affecting governing institutions, particularly at the federal level, was spotted by a few scholars decades ago. A 1976 report by Robert Teeter showed "tremendously increasing rates" of public alienation from, and cynicism about, government.[4] Teeter traced this change in attitudes back to the late 1960s. His findings were confirmed in a 2015 Pew report, which found that "the share [of Americans] saying they could trust the federal government to do the right thing nearly always or most of the time reached an all-time high of 77% in 1964. Within a decade . . . trust had fallen by more than half, to 36%. By the end of the 1970s, only about a quarter of Americans felt that they could trust the government at least most of the time."[5] This decline would grow even more as we entered the 21st century.

Public trust in government: 1958-2015

Trust the federal government to do what is right just about always/most of the time ...

Trust in government has been declining since the mid-1960s. This graph shows the percentage of the public who "trust the federal government to do what is right always/most of the time."

Why have attitudes changed so much? Could it be that these changes are related to people's concern that control over their lives has been slowly slipping out of their hands? Today, many Americans feel powerless to influence, affect, or even communicate, not just with governments but with many large governing institutions.[6] This sense of powerlessness brings with it frustration and anger. For some time, citizens have felt relegated to the sidelines, where they sit uncertain about their ability to make a difference in their own democracy.[7] "Citizen," as the term is employed throughout this report, is used in the sense of *all* the people who live in, care about, and are willing to work to improve a community and the country. They are the *demos* or collective citizenry in "democracy."

Because it has been growing for decades, I believe that the public's dissatisfaction with its governing institutions isn't likely to end quickly. Furthermore, it isn't confined to the United States; it threatens other countries as well.[8] And now, the tone has changed in alarming ways. Frustration and anger have turned into sharp bitterness as the political environment has become supercharged with hyper-partisanship, which has spread onto our Main Streets. Making matters worse, some professionals in the governing institutions have little confidence in the public. The distrust is mutual.[9]

A House Divided?

Loss of confidence in institutions has been compounded by a tidal wave of divisiveness in society. This divisiveness pits people against one another as enemies; it takes many forms and is highly contagious. While there are some constructive initiatives, less is being said today about forgiveness, reconciliation, and loving your enemies. Thomas Hobbes comes to mind: Are we entering the worst of all worlds where there is a war of all against all?[10] Remember Abraham Lincoln's warning: "A house divided against itself cannot stand."[11] About the only thing everybody agrees on is that there is too much divisiveness.[12] And despite the divisions, there is some evidence of a growing common ground on certain policies.[13]

Democracy Itself Is in Trouble

Democracies have never been trouble-free, but they are resilient. Their most serious difficulties are fundamental ones of democracy itself, which keep it from functioning as it should. The mechanisms for self-rule have malfunctioned because of deep-seated problems behind the obvious problems. We face these kinds of problems today; they are compounded by structural dysfunctions in areas like racial, ethnic, and gender relationships. Adding to these difficulties, even while democracy is valued by a solid majority, there are those who no longer believe in it.[14] Alarmingly, this is more the case with some young people.

When I grew up, during World War II, democracy wasn't a contested value because Americans knew what the alternative would be—dictatorial authoritarianism. Most people today realize that democracy is facing serious difficulties, but even if they feel it is up to them to do something (which they do), they aren't sure what they can do or whether they can count on their fellow citizens. Furthermore, a recent survey concluded that "Americans have no strong, clear sense of what a healthy, civically engaged democracy entails."[15]

Because the loss of public confidence in governing institutions is so serious in a democracy, there have already been efforts to counter it. How effective have they been?

Does "Public Engagement" Engage the Public?

Terms for measures to improve the relationship between the citizenry and governing institutions vary: *public participation, civic engagement, consultation, public accountability*. Regrettably, declining public confidence hasn't been arrested by decades of these efforts. Even more alarming, many participatory practices may be counterproductive, unintentionally widening the divide that they were intended to close.[16] Whether or not this is the case, the loss of public confidence has increased even as engagement efforts have grown.

Many Americans have difficulty seeing a place for "people like me" in highly professionalized, bureaucratized governing institutions.*

I don't mean to dismiss totally the usual remedies for countering the loss of public confidence. When I worked in the federal government, I encouraged using them. They have value. Yet I have come to the conclusion that they don't go far enough.

WHY NOT TRY MORE GOVERNING *WITH*?

Maybe there are other strategies for dealing with the public's alienation that need to be tested. One possibility is captured in the word *with*. The idea behind a *with* strategy was inspired by Abraham Lincoln's ideal of a government *of*, *by*, and *for* the people in the Gettysburg Address. Today, do Americans think our government as "of" the people? That's debatable. "By" the people? Doubtful. "For" the people? Perhaps for some, sometimes. So why not add another preposition—governing *with* the people? Maybe that would help bridge the divide separating the people of the United States from their government and from many of the country's major institutions. Fortunately, we already have some cases of this happening, which I will discuss later. I am suggesting that we build on these cases to create a different form of collaboration that would have all governing institutions working more *with* citizens, not just *for* them. In fact, I believe that working *with* citizens is the best way of working *for* them.

What I am proposing isn't a sweeping, fix-everything-now solution. It is rather an incremental, build-on-what-grows strategy that could have a cumulative effect on the troubles our democracy faces. A *with* strategy doesn't have a model to copy or a set of best practices to follow. It's just a different way of thinking about the relationship citizens should have with their governing institutions.

---

* In 2017, a Bosque County, Texas, resident put it this way: "They [the leaders of the political system] don't care about *people like me*" (emphasis added). Laurie Kellman and Emily Swanson, "AP-NORC Poll: Three-Quarters in US Say They Lack Influence," Associated Press, July 12, 2017.

At the dedication of the Gettysburg National Cemetery on November 19, 1863, Abraham Lincoln closed his address with these words: "[T]his nation, under God, shall have a new birth of freedom—and that government of the people, by the people, for the people, shall not perish from the earth."

The proper application of any such concept is a challenging question because there is no one certain, correct answer. What is important is not allowing this uncertainty to obscure the value of the idea. A different way of thinking is useful because it can open doors to imagining new ways of acting. And opening doors may have more to do with the character of the relationships between citizens and institutions and the spirit in which collaboration occurs than it does with changes in organizational structure.

A Democratic Strategy

A *with* strategy is, most of all, a strategy for strengthening our democracy. Saying that, of course, demands an explanation of what is meant by *democracy* in this report, because the word has many meanings. The most common is that democracy is a system of contested elections resulting in a representative government. Democracy can also mean the institutions of the government: courts, legislatures, and administrative agencies. These are certainly valid definitions. Less precise, "democracy" is just the way things are in the country. And because some people don't like the way things are, they say they don't like "democracy."

More troubling, a good many people don't think of democracy as *us*. It's somebody else—maybe the politicians, maybe those who lead the institutions, but it's not you and me. A strong democracy has to be "us." That understanding of democracy was captured in a theme from the Civil Rights Movement: "We are the ones we've been waiting for." This concept of democracy may have lost some of its traction today. Yet in the most profound sense, *We* the People, *are* the democracy. That idea is at the heart of a *with* strategy.

I think what we now call democracy began long before the word itself was used. It grew out of lessons taken from the collective actions needed for human survival when our ancestors were hunter-gatherers living in bands, tribal enclaves, and, later, villages. This was before there were kingdoms and nation-states.[17] As humans spread out around the globe, they carried with them a "political DNA" developed in the struggle to survive. A principal lesson of survival was that cooperation is key because we needed to work together, even with those from different bands or tribes, in order to stay alive. The first *with* strategy was people working *with* people.

Much, much later, the ancient Greeks captured some of this survival legacy in their language with terms like *democracy*. This word has two roots. I've already mentioned the first: *demos*, "the citizenry or the people collectively" as in a village or *deme*. The second is *kratos*, "sovereign power," which implies the capacity to act with authority in ways that make a real difference.[18] Modern representative government rests on this earlier civic foundation of shared decision-making leading to common actions taken for our common well-being.

From this perspective, democracy is both a way of life and a political system in which, at the most fundamental or organic level, citizens must work with other citizens to produce things—"public goods"—that make life better for everyone. Our ancestors went on to form governments and other governing institutions to create more and different public goods. These two systems, one governmental or institutional and the other organic or civic, are interdependent in the ecosystem of democracy. (That is the subject of an earlier Kettering Foundation Press book, *The Ecology of Democracy*.[19]) Unfortunately, this essential, symbiotic relationship becomes weaker if citizens don't join to produce public goods, if they delegate much of what they must do to governing institutions, or if these institutions are influenced wholly by professional expertise and bureaucratic practices. Any of these relegates citizens to the sidelines.

A *With* Legacy

Although a *with* strategy is idealistic in that it is democratic, it isn't a pie-in-the-sky fantasy. The United States has long recognized the need for what citizens provide with laws allowing tax exemptions for nongovernmental institutions serving a public purpose.[20] And public-government interaction is, in fact, very common in some situations. Think about communities hit by natural disasters—fires, floods, and storms. Research has shown that in the first days after disaster strikes, survival depends largely on people assisting people: "successful remedies and recovery for communitywide disasters are neither conceived nor implemented solely by trained emergency personnel, nor are they confined to preauthorized procedures." This comes from a study that found, "family members, friends, coworkers, neighbors, and strangers who happen to be in the vicinity often carry out search and rescue activities and provide medical aid before police, fire, and other officials even arrive on the scene."[21]

Yet, although collaboration with government agencies does occur in such extreme circumstances, it isn't a well-established policy.

A *with* strategy is also implicit in everyday examples of people working with people, not only among those who are alike or who like one another, but among those who recognize they *need* one another to live the lives they want to live.

Reciprocity and Complementary Production

"Working *with*" is based on reciprocity, and reciprocity makes me think of a scene from my childhood. Where I am from, pine trees grow so rapidly that they are treated as a crop like corn, which is harvested and replanted. Today, seedlings are set out in neat rows so the timber can be gathered easily by machines. But before this equipment was available, the trees were cut by long crosscut saws, with two workers reciprocating in pulling the blade back and forth. Their efforts produced a result that neither laborer could have achieved by working alone. They worked *with* each other.

A crosscut saw is used to cut a felled tree into sections as part of a "Logs for Victory" drive sponsored by the War Production Board during World War II.

A *with* strategy fosters reciprocity between what citizens do on their end of the "saw" and what governing institutions do on the other end.* The strategy is based on evidence that most major institutions can't do their jobs as effectively without the complementary efforts of people working *with* people.[22] That is because there are some things that can only be done by citizens or that are best done by them.

The case for complementary efforts was made persuasively in Elinor Ostrom's Nobel Prize-winning research on what she called "coproduction." Citizens can't be left on the sidelines, she said, because their work is needed to reinforce and complete the work of governments, schools, and other institutions. Here is Ostrom's very practical argument:

> If one presumes that teachers produce education, police produce safety, doctors and nurses produce health, and social workers produce effective households, the focus of attention is on how to professionalize the public service. Obviously, skilled teachers, police officers, medical personnel, and social workers are essential to the development of better public services. Ignoring the important role of children, families, support groups, neighborhood organizations, and churches in the production of these services means, however, that only a portion of the inputs to these processes are taken into account in the way that policy makers think about these problems. The term "client" is used more and more frequently to refer to those who should be viewed as essential co-producers of their own education, safety, health, and communities. A client is the name for a passive role. Being a co-producer makes one an active partner.[23]

Products from the work of citizens can complete what institutions do because civic work is different from the work of institutions. Yet even when the work is the same, the effects of the work are different

---

*   Robert Putnam makes this same point in his work on social capital, finding that "a society that relies on generalized reciprocity is more efficient than a distrustful society." Robert Putnam, "The Prosperous Community: Social Capital and Public Life," *The American Prospect*, December 19, 2001.

depending on who does it. My neighbors cleaning up and clearing the road to our houses has a different effect than when a city crew does it. Neighbors working with neighbors builds a sense of community.

That acknowledged, I want to focus now on the projects that make use of people doing the things professionals don't—and sometimes can't—do. That's why I prefer the term *complementary production* rather than *coproduction*.

A good example of complementary production is captured in a story a colleague told me about an exchange between a group of citizens in her community and their local government. The citizens had initiated a cultural project, but when they met with municipal officials they didn't ask them to take over the project. They simply asked, "Here is what we have done. Now what can you do?" Town officials then offered assistance, using resources that the citizens didn't have. This is the type of reciprocity that is central to a *with* strategy. Citizens take an initiative; they work together to make the things (public goods) that serve the common good. Then a governing institution adds the resources it has.

Things Only Citizens Can Do

I want to emphasize that complementary production is essential because there are things that can *only* be done by citizens working with citizens. Public institutions in a democracy can't create their own legitimacy. They can't, on their own, define their purposes or set the standards by which they will operate. And governing institutions can't sustain over the long term decisions that citizens are unwilling to support. Governments can build common highways but not common ground. And none of the governing institutions—even the most powerful—can generate the public determination required to keep a community or country moving ahead on difficult problems. This determination is necessary for attacking those problems that grow out of a lack of community and then destroy that community. Also, only citizens have the local knowledge that comes from living in a place 365 days a year. Because of this knowledge, people know how to do things that are different from what professionals can and should do. Finally, large institutions, governmental and nongovernmental, can't create citizens—at least not democratic citizens capable of governing themselves.

What Isn't Being Proposed

A *with* strategy isn't simply another form of public participation. And at the federal level, it doesn't just mean partnering with state and local governments. A *with* strategy also goes beyond consulting with citizens who are beneficiaries of programs. Moreover, it isn't the same as transferring government responsibilities to nongovernmental organizations; it isn't devolution. And it is more than volunteers serving institutions like schools and hospitals, valuable as that is. I am not critical of any of these efforts or alliances, yet I believe more of the things only citizens can provide must be added. I am joining the Ostrom chorus.

FROM DOUBT TO RESPECT

I know there are obstacles to a *with* strategy. And I want to recognize them. Some have to do with the governing institutions. Does the way they work allow them to collaborate with citizens as producers, not just as clients or "customers"? And then there are doubts about citizens— their abilities, resources, and political will, all of which are need if people are to do their share of the work that collaboration requires.

Do people have what it takes to assume the responsibilities of self-rule? They are often thought to be apathetic, selfish, uninformed, biased, hopelessly divided, and easily manipulated. These are just a few of the charges. The hard truth is that many of these criticisms are justified; human beings have all of these failings and more. Yet that isn't the whole story. Citizens can also be brave, generous, helpful, compassionate, and self-sacrificing. That is a long list, too. It isn't uncommon for people who differ one day to join forces the next when confronted with a threat to their common well-being, even crossing historical lines of division or facing considerable risk to do so.

Why then the different behaviors, particularly when talking about the same people? Why selfish one day and self-sacrificing another? A full explanation goes beyond the scope of this report, but I raise the question to make the point that negative feelings about our fellow citizens can obscure the more constructive things people do.

Seeing Citizens as Producers

Whatever the complete explanation may be, one answer to the question about these differences may have to do with how people understand their role as citizens. Do citizens just obey laws, pay taxes, and vote? Is that all? Even in participatory projects, people may think of themselves as merely constituents to be heard or consumers to receive services. Citizens become those who are acted upon rather than actors or agents themselves.

I am suggesting another role for citizens, as producers, people who make things to benefit the common good. I realize this concept of citizenship isn't the conventional one, yet I was encouraged when the World Economic Forum, an organization of business leaders, issued a report that recognized the value of citizens being regarded as creators and producers rather than just consumers or clients.[24] A *with* strategy sees citizens as producers.

Developing a Sense of Sovereignty

How do people come to think of themselves as producers? History may offer one answer. Consider what happened after the American Revolution and the adoption of state constitutions, which were made necessary by the Revolution.

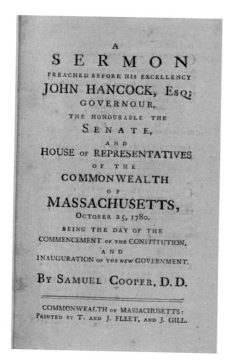

A

SERMON

PREACHED BEFORE HIS EXCELLENCY

JOHN HANCOCK, Esq;

GOVERNOUR,

THE HONOURABLE THE

SENATE,

AND

HOUSE OF REPRESENTATIVES

OF THE

COMMONWEALTH

OF

MASSACHUSETTS,

OCTOBER 25, 1780.

BEING THE DAY OF THE

COMMENCEMENT OF THE CONSTITUTION,

AND

INAUGURATION OF THE NEW GOVERNMENT.

BY SAMUEL COOPER, D. D.

COMMONWEALTH OF MASSACHUSETTS:
PRINTED BY T. AND J. FLEET, AND J. GILL.

{ 27 }

subject to no laws, by which you do not consent to bind yourselves. In such an attitude human nature appears with it's proper dignity: On such a basis, life, and all that sweetens and adorns it, may rest with as much security as human imperfection can possibly admit: In such a constitution we find a country deserving to be loved, and worthy to be defended. For what is our country? Is it a soil of which, tho' we may be the present possessors, we can call no part our own? or the air in which we first drew our breath, from which we may be confined in a dungeon, or of which we may be deprived by the ax or the halter at the pleasure of a tyrant? Is not a country a constitution—an established frame of laws; of which a man may say, "we are here united in society for our common security and happiness. These fields and these fruits are my own: The regulations under which I live are my own; I am not only a proprietor in the soil, but I am part of the sovereignty of my country". Such ought to be the community of men, and such, adored be the goodness of the supreme Ruler of the world, such, at present is our own country; of which this day affords a bright evidence, a glorious recognition. E 2   To

Samuel Cooper's sermon.

After the victory over the British, Samuel Cooper, a Boston minister sympathetic to the American rebels, gave a sermon in 1780 at a ceremony recognizing the creation, after lengthy public debate, of a new constitution for Massachusetts. He compared the constitution that had been passed to the fruits that farmers produce by their labor. Cooper reasoned that the Revolution had spawned a new framework of laws—"the regulations under which I live." This meant that the victorious rebels he was addressing were entitled to claim, "I am not only a proprietor in the soil, but *I am part of the sovereignty of my country*" (emphasis added).[25] Cooper's generation had a right to this sense of sovereignty because they had, in fact, been instrumental in creating not just a new state constitution but a new nation. Our actions can not only change our circumstances, they can change us by altering how we see ourselves.

Generating Power and Responsibility

The voluntary work of producing things for the common good, whether constitutions or, today, neighborhood playgrounds, can generate a sense of sovereignty. This sense is both one of power and accomplishment, as well as one of responsibility. Human beings are likely to take more responsibility for what they have made than what is made for them. They are motivated by necessity; people need constitutions and playgrounds. But when citizens create these things, it shows them that they are powerful, that they can make a difference. I would add that this power that comes from working *with* others is different from the power that is coercively exercised *over* others. Power *with* has been the key to human survival since humans have been on the planet. And it is this power that a *with* strategy generates.

Power *with* also helps counter the loss of public confidence in institutions. When people have worked *with* an institution to solve a problem, they tend to have positive feelings about it, provided that the institution has been receptive and the work wasn't just menial. When people have favorable opinions about schools, for example, they may speak as agents, saying, "*Ours* is a good school." Then they often add, "And we are involved in it." Seeing this connection helped me recognize the possibility of restoring confidence in governing institutions by using a *with* strategy.

Deliberating to Exercise Sound Judgment

Our earliest human ancestors would not have lasted long in their dangerous world without the ability to make good decisions about how to protect themselves and find the resources they needed to stay alive. We humans survived by the collective decision-making that led to productive collective action. As a result, over time, our brains became hard wired for shared decision-making.* As individuals, our brains also have biases that lead to mistakes. However, deciding with others can counter these biases when there is a diversity of experiences to inform our decision-making. (Without this diversity, a collection of individuals can become a mob.) We have a faculty for making sound judgments with others that will, if we use it, help us avoid mistakes individuals are susceptible to making. Public deliberation is a process for exercising this faculty as a citizenry. It involves carefully weighing, together, the worth of competing possibilities for collective action.

Our ancestors would have used some collective body, perhaps a village gathering, to make important decisions. These days, a community might make decisions in a council meeting. And citizens are also likely to begin deliberating in the places where they routinely gather—in clubs, religious institutions, coffee shops, and even around kitchen tables. Wherever it is done, deliberative decision-making involves looking at the pros and cons of various options in order to find a path for moving forward.

Naming Problems Deliberation begins by choosing names that identify common problems. When people encounter a problem, they describe it, which is what I mean by giving it a name. The names people give to problems tend to reflect the various things they have long considered deeply valuable—their security (including food), their freedom to forage wherever they need to go, and their being treated fairly in the distribution of the goods made by working together. Most of all, people want the control needed to get what they considered most valuable.

Considering the Options The various things we hold dear lead to various options for action. To make sound decisions, we have to put all of the options or proposals for action on the table. This creates a

---

* In their review of the neurobiology of decision-making, Ernst and Paulus explain how deliberative decision-making is integrated into the neurological process. In scientific terms, deliberation is closely associated with the functions of the right dorsolateral cortex and the orbitofrontal cortex. Other parts of the brain contribute emotional processing, which is critical in deliberation. Monique Ernst and Martin P. Paulus, "Neurobiology of Decision Making: A Selective Review from a Neurocognitive and Clinical Perspective," *Biological Psychiatry* 58, no. 8 (2005): 597-604.

framework for deliberative decision-making. A framework, however, is just the scaffolding for what needs to be done next.

What can be most difficult for people trying to deliberate is to give a "fair trial" to all options, even those that some may have reason to oppose. Admittedly, recognizing what is good in an option that is labeled as "bad" is a challenge. Nonetheless, it's imperative to hear opposing views. An unpopular or minority opinion may contain information or surface feelings that have to be taken into consideration if a decision is to serve the good of all.

Recognizing Tensions Because people consider many different things valuable, there will inevitably be tensions. There are downsides to any actions we might want to take—no free lunches. What makes us secure, for example, can also restrict our freedom. Deliberation helps us work through these tensions, not until we all agree, but to the point we can see what we can and can't live with.

Realizing that the tensions are among things that are valuable to everyone helps change the decision-making from one of people against people to people against a shared problem. When deliberating, people don't necessarily come to agree with or like one another, yet they can see that others, however mistaken they may appear to be, are not evil. The tone of the decision-making becomes less toxic and divisive. And that is no small benefit when people have to work together to overcome a problem.

Doing Choice Work Dealing with the pulls and tugs of tensions is hard to do. It's tempting to avoid it out of fear of conflict, yet people can deliberate to get this work done. Deliberating is natural; individuals do it all the time when they have big decisions to make. But public deliberating, often with strangers, is actual work, "choice work" some call it. Because it requires considerable effort, deliberating is more than having informed and civil discussions. We have to move beyond hasty reactions and exercise our faculty for judgment if we are going to make sound decisions.

Can everyone deliberate? Like any form of work, choice work takes practice. That is true of many things that are natural. However, based on decades of reports from the deliberative National Issues Forums, differences in educational level or economic status don't appear to be impediments.*

Avoiding Misunderstandings about Deliberations I've gone into detail about deliberative decision-making because there are a variety of meanings for the term *deliberation* these days. It's no wonder that there is some confusion about the kind discussed here, which has been mistaken for purely rational, fact-based decision-making.

Certainly, factual information is essential. However, because many political questions are about what is the *right* thing to do and facts alone aren't enough, people have to rely on the moral reasoning that deliberation employs. Moral reasoning recognizes that questions of what is right arouse strong emotions, and deliberation helps people come to terms with those feelings.

Because of the importance placed on facts and data, it is frequently assumed that only the well-educated can deliberate. That just isn't so. People from all walks of life have taken part in public deliberations, and there have been no reports of any groups that lacked the capacity for this choice work. Professor Bonnie Braun and a research team at the University of Maryland studied forums involving women from poor, rural communities. Their research did not show any lack of capacity for deliberating.[26]

Another point of confusion is to think of deliberating as a series of steps to be taken in a prescribed order. First name a problem, then lay out options, and so on. I realize that I have contributed to this confusion in the way I have broken deliberation into distinct

---

* The National Issues Forums are local deliberations sponsored by a network of independent, nonpartisan organizations ranging from libraries to schools to civic organizations. The forums have been going on nationwide for about 40 years. Many of them were partners with USA TODAY in its coverage prior to the 2020 elections. Kettering research is used in preparing issue guides to start some of these deliberations. "Hidden Common Ground Health Care," *USA TODAY,* February 7-9, 2020. Information on NIF issue guides (based on Kettering Research) is available through the National Issues Forums Institute at www.nifi.org.

components to describe it. The fact is that people constantly go back and forth. When identifying options to consider, they may realize that the name they have given the problem is inaccurate or incomplete. And wrestling with tensions can lead people to add or modify options. Public decision-making is not neatly linear.

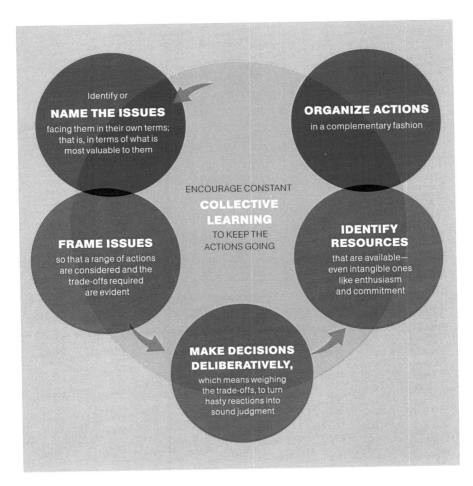

Deliberating isn't a series of steps to be taken in a prescribed order. People constantly go back and forth between naming, framing, deciding, identifying resources, organizing action, and learning.

Public deliberation is also easily misunderstood when it is not seen as natural but rather as one of the many techniques used in small groups. The misperception that deliberation requires special skills that only a few have often comes from seeing that working through tensions is difficult. But everything that is natural isn't necessarily easy. There is no doubt that this kind of deliberation requires hard choice work. This is why civil, informed discussion isn't enough to produce deliberation. People have to face up to unpleasant trade-offs to trigger the brain to exercise its faculty for judgment.

Perhaps the most common misperception is that deliberation is just talk, not action. Politics is certainly about action and so is deliberation. It is the decision-making about *how* to act. You may have noticed that I have a fondness for the ancient Greek language. It described deliberation as the talk (*logo*) used before people act in order to first teach themselves (*prodidacthenai*) how to act.[27] Deliberative decision-making is intertwined with acting. The experience of acting continually shapes the decision-making, just as the decision-making shapes the action.[28] Thinking of deliberation as separate from action makes no sense.

Still another misconception has to do with the deliberative forums where participants aren't chosen but are self-selected. Participants may be demographically alike, so the assumption is that they all think alike. This isn't what we've seen. In deliberating, demographic alikes often discover that they have quite different opinions. Also, although people do take comfort in opinions they admire, they may also be curious about contrary views, provided those views aren't advanced in an offensive manner. People certainly try to persuade one another as they hold on to cherished beliefs. Yet, as they deliberate, people can begin to reevaluate even the options they like best.

Some critics say that deliberation is OK, but it is limited to highly structured forums, and that, as such, it will never "get up to scale." Yes, formally organized forums are limited to a certain number of people and certain places. Furthermore, all forums aren't deliberative and all deliberations aren't in forums. That said, the role of forums is to help people distinguish deliberation from other forms of speech and to take what they learn into the deliberative system that is part of everyday speech. Champions of deliberation certainly want their forums to "get up to scale." Yet, in a sense, deliberation is already up to scale because some form of it goes on every day, particularly in our personal lives. The challenge isn't to invent deliberation, it is to improve it for use in our public lives.

Learning Together Let me add a word about the importance of "teaching ourselves," or learning together. Collective learning is a democratic way of making change. It is different from the planning that institutions use to direct change. (More about that shortly.) The power in deliberative learning comes from combining a range of experience, which helps people develop a more comprehensive sense of the realities they face. Hannah Arendt, drawing upon the German philosopher Immanuel Kant, called this comprehensive sense an "enlarged mentality," the ability to see things from others' points of view.[29] Furthermore, communities where people continue to learn together are more likely to be resilient and persist even when their efforts don't succeed at first. In these communities, failure becomes an opportunity for learning.

Everyday Opportunities Opportunities for public deliberating are visible every day in community routines. There are numerous opportunities for citizens to turn these routines into empowering democratic practices. For instance, problems are constantly being named by political leaders and professionals. Citizens can add their names, showing what is deeply valuable to them. They can also include options for action that draw on their resources of experiences, skills, and associations. Citizens can certainly hold their own deliberations in community organizations like libraries and civic clubs. Many of these organizations—like Osher Lifelong Learning Institutes—sponsor explicitly deliberative forums. And they can add to evaluations what they are learning from community programs, projects, and problem-solving initiatives.

People deliberating in an NIF forum.

Using Resources Available to Citizens

Even if citizens have the ability to deliberate, do they have the resources to implement their decisions? People typically look for the kinds of resources that institutions have, such as money. (The hunt for funding has stopped more civic initiatives than any tyrant ever has.) Funding isn't unimportant, and I don't mean to dismiss it. Yet people have other resources, which can go untapped because they aren't recognized.* Those resources are often in communities. In fact, communities themselves can be resources.

Communities as Power   Much of the work citizens do as producers begins locally. And more attention is now being given to the importance of communities and what citizens can do there. Writers James and Deborah Fallows toured communities across

---

* Another reason that resources go unrecognized and unused is that people aren't looking for them. Resources become valuable assets when people see them as useful in making the difference they want to make politically but don't think they have the power. Even pointing out resources isn't likely to be effective if that isn't the context.

America from 2013 to 2016 and reported that, while many news stories gave the impression that the country was "going to hell," the view locally was usually positive.[30] "The closer [people] are to the action at home, the better they like what they see."[31] Perhaps this is a result of frustration with Washington, yet, whatever the reasons, constructive change at the community level appears more likely. That said, community politics is not immune to the partisan polarization that infects national politics.

Communities have a great many resources in numerous areas. In health, they can be stocked with the "medicine" of human compassion that comes from family, friends, and neighbors. Institutions can care *for* people but not *about* them in the way that people can. In addition to family and friends, larger "networks of nurture" organized by communities can be a potent force in combating the behavioral and social problems that contribute to many illnesses.[32] This has been demonstrated in research done for the Centers for Disease Control and Prevention, which shows that community care can reduce the incidence of heart disease, strokes, and lung cancer.[33] Once underappreciated, other studies also document the healing powers of community care.[34] This care is also vital in providing for the social welfare of vulnerable citizens.

Communities have also been important in the education of children because, in addition to schools, most have an array of other educating institutions, from libraries and museums to clubs for young people, not to mention religious institutions and families. And in economic development, communities are now listed along with capital, labor, and technology as critical factors because their social norms transfer to the factory floor.[35]

Associations as Power Another powerful resource citizens have is in the associations they create, which connect individual skills and experiences into an armada of assets. Some of the most effective of these groups are at the grassroots level. John McKnight has spent a career studying civic associations, particularly in neighborhoods.[36]

He points out that these groups provide care for the vulnerable young and elderly, as well as people with disabilities. They develop leadership as well because everyone has to play a role. These associations are problem solvers. They also encourage initiative and enterprise. Most significant of all, John reminds us that associating is different from voting, which delegates power to others. Associating *generates* power.

The importance of associations was made further evident in a 2018 study of what has allowed some cities to lower their crime rates when others couldn't.[37] These cities had generators of civic energy in a multitude of associations of citizens working together to improve their community. Researchers found that "every 10 additional [civic] organizations in a city with 100,000 residents . . . led to a 9 percent drop in the murder rate and a 6 percent drop in violent crime."[38] These civic groups didn't necessarily regard their work as preventing violence, but "in creating playgrounds, they enabled parents to better monitor their children. In connecting neighbors, they improved the capacity of residents to control their streets. In forming after-school programs, they offered alternatives to crime."[39] Even if not directly related to crime, these efforts helped turn negative emotions into positive energy.

The associations citizens organize often begin as small, informal coalitions of people who share common concerns. These small "cells" are like the microorganisms that are essential to life on the planet. They can respond quickly to problems because they are citizen led, not bureaucratic. Small groups become even more effective when they are loosely connected in networks with other small groups.

A word of caution: Associations, especially primary grassroots ones, have been so effective at dealing with social problems that grantmakers, large nongovernmental civic organizations, and governments try to help them. This can unintentionally result in the small associations taking on the bureaucratic features of the larger organizations. They become "colonized" by the institutions, which can result in robbing the grassroots organizations of the authenticity that makes them so effective.*

---

* The ill effects of colonization on informal civic associations became apparent to some grantmaking foundations when they realized that their grants weren't working. In studying why, the Kettering

Civic associations have helped to lower crime rates in some cities by creating playgrounds and offering after-school programs.

Although institutions organize actions centrally and bureaucratically, the associations citizens form can act in varied and less formal ways. And if their actions share broad, general purposes (identified through deliberation), they can reinforce one another. When that happens, it makes the sum of the civic efforts much greater than the individual parts.

CAN GOVERNING INSTITUTIONS WORK *WITH* CITIZENS?

While many people may not be certain about what citizens can do, they probably know a great deal about what institutions do, especially governments. So I don't see a need to elaborate here. However, what goes on *inside* the governing institutions—in their bureaucracies— can be a mystery. Inviting people to look at what happens inside

---

Foundation noticed that these foundations typically have distinct ways of going about their business that aren't suited to the often ad hoc associations citizens use when they solve problems. In Kettering's report on its findings, institutions (governmental and philanthropic) were called "Squares" and the grassroots civic associations, "Blobs." The creator of TimeBanking, Edgar Cahn, picked up on this distinction in his book, *No More Throw-Away People*, and turned Kettering's findings into a very clever animation, "The Parable of the Blobs and Squares." The video can be viewed at https://vimeo.com/42332617.

a bureaucracy can be like inviting them into the proverbial meat-packing plant where sausage is ground. I certainly don't want to join the chorus of "ughs" that this analogy provokes. Having worked in several bureaucracies, I am often asked to explain why bureaucracies do what they do. There are many complexities, and I won't go into all of them in this report. In brief, here is the best explanation I have.

Governing and large nongoverning institutions like schools and hospitals rely on bureaucracies. If there is to be collaboration with a public that is willing to collaborate, most of it will have to occur between citizens and bureaucracies. The question is, can those governing these governing institutions carry out a *with* strategy? Why should that even be a question? After all, bureaucrats are our fellow citizens. Yet, these citizens play a different role when they are in their professions. Judges are citizens, but when they are on the bench, we address them as "Your Honor."

Differences in roles are part of the answer in explaining why governing institutions act the way they do, but that doesn't fully account for why carrying out a *with* strategy can be difficult. There are situations when professionals and citizens work together. Disaster recovery is one. And Ostrom's evidence for the benefits of coproduction should appeal to the self-interests of governing institutions. What then are the obstacles?

It Isn't Incompetence

A popular explanation for why bureaucracies have trouble working with citizens is a mirror image of the criticism of citizens, which is that bureaucratic behavior is the result of incompetence or, worse, not caring. I don't think that explanation holds water. Most of the professional administrators I've met have been conscientious about doing a good job and well prepared to carry out their responsibilities. However, administrators often have serious reservations about what citizens can offer because they don't have the training that professionals have. And there is little recognition of what citizens can do that institutions can't. People sense this lack of respect, and it is another, more serious obstacle to a productive relationship with bureaucracies.

Bureaucratism and Professionalism

Many Americans don't feel they have any meaningful influence on governing institutions, and some believe that bureaucracies take away what little control they have left over their lives. Are administrators really intent on taking away people's control and denying them any influence? I don't think so. What is happening is more complex. I believe it has to do with the cultures inside institutions, which I call "–isms." These cultures prevent or undercut meaningful collaboration with the citizenry. Furthermore, these cultures have become integrated, with the result that they are much more powerful.

Bureaucratism Bureaucracies provide order and structure. They combat favoritism with their uniform application of rules. Most of us have some bureaucratic propensities in us; we need order and structure in our lives. These are just some of the reasons why bureaucracies have been around a long time and aren't likely to go away.

The first bureaucracies were created in ancient cities, like those in Mesopotamia and Egypt.[40] Historically, their authority came from of the heads of states, monarchs of some type. Bureaucrats carried out royal decrees, and to back up this authority, the monarchs' ministers had coercive powers. That history created an influential culture in bureaucracies that I've called "bureaucratism" to emphasize that I am not talking about individuals.

Professionalism Professionalism is different from bureaucratism; in fact, it is quite modern. This culture is no longer dependent on a monarch or even on democratic leaders. Authority comes from science—objective, verifiable, fact-based "truth."

Professionalism gave us public administration, a field that came out of the Civil Service reforms of the late 19th century and the proposals of scholars like Woodrow Wilson (who would go on to become president). Wilson wanted the work of expert administrators

There are situations when professionals and citizens already work with one another,

to be objective and divorced from politics. That, however, created a tension with democracy, which Wilson recognized. This tension remains.

Public administration's effort to rise above venal politics failed to anticipate other influences, such as that coming from a growing number of interest groups. Nonetheless, reformers believed that scientific expertise should guide the ship of state and replace the favoritism and the winner-take-all spoils system for appointing government employees.

The science of professionalism brought with it a way of reasoning that inclined institutions to "see like a state."[41] Context and idiosyncratic circumstances became less visible in policy considerations. The values of the new professional system were also different from those in the old system. Responsiveness, a feature of the old system, wasn't as important as uniformity and impartiality.[42]

When professionalized institutions see like a state, it can give the public the impression that the bureaucrats who work in them lack common sense.[43] I recall such a case from when I was Secretary of

including disaster recovery. Here, citizens clear rubble in the aftermath of a tornado.

the Department of Health, Education, and Welfare, when the policy of an institution clashed with what most people thought was a no-brainer. In this instance, a grandmother was told that she could not be away from her nursing home to spend Christmas with her family because she would exceed a 14-day limit on absences from the facility.

From most people's perspective, it was obvious that the woman would be better off with her family. From an institutional policy perspective, however, consistency ruled. Allowing someone to break the rules would make it impossible to refuse other such requests. Furthermore, the health care provided in the grandmother's nursing home was the most expensive kind, and the government was paying the bill. The 14-day rule was based on the premise that someone who could be absent for two weeks didn't actually need the expensive care. The policy couldn't "see" the fluctuation in the grandmother's condition that her family could. Her health varied from month-to-month. She needed nursing care sometimes, but that Christmas she was fine. Although working *with* the family was medically desirable, it wasn't possible. (The grandmother's appeal reached my desk and she spent Christmas with her family. Rules have to be tempered with judgment.)

The Combination of Forces Ancient bureaucratism and modern professionalism have combined in today's institutions, allowing the two cultures to reinforce one another and become even more influential. One result has been an increase in the independence of bureaucracies from elected officials. Bureaucracies in large, nongovernmental institutions may have gained somewhat similar autonomy. In some extreme cases, the independence is justified. Yet a practice of taking authority away from those who have been elected may not restore public confidence.

The argument that professionals should have independent powers has its roots in a debate over whether appointed officials are only meant to carry out the orders of those who are chosen by the people or whether they should have a semiautonomous role, with the power to develop and enforce policies on their own.* The argument for this more assertive role began with the claim that legislative processes are too slow to respond to urgent matters. There may be similar arguments for more autonomy at the operating level in nongovernmental institutions.

Differences in Ways of Working

Perhaps you can see why I find explaining how governing institutions act to be quite complex. Still another explanation for why large institutions act as they do has to do with differences between the way citizens go about their work and the way governing institutions do theirs. Although these differences are justified, they can be significant obstacles to collaboration. Why? After all, the tasks that make up any kind of work are similar. Most involve identifying problems,

---

*   See the literature on the difference between "institutional" and "constitutive" powers for more details. For example, Brian J. Cook's, *Bureaucracy and Self-Government* (Baltimore, MD: Johns Hopkins University Press, 1996).

making decisions about what needs to be done, finding the necessary resources, organizing the efforts, and evaluating what happens.

The differences begin in diagnosing the problems that need to be solved. People don't identify problems in expert terms. They are influenced by the things that humans consider valuable: their security, freedom, and the other things they hold dear. People also draw on the local knowledge that comes from years of direct experience with problems. And the options for actions to solve these problems go beyond the things that can be done by institutions alone. Citizens act through their families, civic associations, and social networks. Also, the resources citizens draw on to act, such as personal skills and experiences, are different from institutional resources. What is more, when citizens make decisions about which options to choose, they don't employ institutional methods like cost-benefit analysis, but, in the best case, use public deliberations. People also organize their work less bureaucratically than institutions. And they can evaluate results differently using the things they hold valuable as standards rather than only quantitative measures.

A BETTER ALIGNMENT

Despite these differences, I still believe that governing institutions and the citizenry can work effectively together by realigning their respective ways of working so that they are mutually reinforcing. This realignment doesn't depend on overhauling established ways of working. Neither regular citizens nor professionals have to do something different; they just have to consider doing what they do differently. That can allow different ways of working to mesh better.

First, how citizens go about their work has to be recognized and respected by governing institutions. As noted, citizens and institutions alike give names to problems, but the terms aren't identical. For example, citizens want to feel that they are safe in their homes, and this feeling of security is less quantifiable yet more compelling to them than the statistics professionals use to describe crime. As people decide what to do about their problems, they also draw on their experiences, not just data. Admittedly, experiences can be misleading, yet the memories of the experiences reflect what people consider valuable. It shouldn't be too difficult for professionals to recognize what is valuable and incorporate the names people use when describing problems. That would be a better alignment.

Some of the best opportunities for a better alignment occur when citizens and professionals are doing the same thing but doing it differently—for example, deliberating to make decisions. Professionals in governing institutions have to weigh various options against their costs and consequences. They have to consider tensions among the things they consider important as they weigh pros and cons. This is their choice work. Citizens do the same thing, albeit in their own terms, as they deliberate. When institutions, governmental or nongovernmental, sit down with a deliberative citizenry to compare the outcomes of their respective efforts at choice work, they are collaborating *with* one another. (This has actually happened in Hawaii on issues like legalizing gambling.[44])

Former Presidents Gerald R. Ford and Jimmy Carter, and David Mathews, listen as a citizen reports on what people said in National Issues Forums on Social Security reform.

THE COSTS OF WORKING *WITH* CITIZENS

Despite potential benefits to citizens, professionals, and democracy itself, a better alignment may still pose risks and have costs for administrators. Citizens need to be aware of this. Professional colleagues may not only fail to be supportive but may be critical. Entering into a collaborative relationship with citizens can also be perilous for administrators if citizens fail to deliver on their share of the work. Consequently, professionals can be hesitant to commit their institutions to collaborate because of this uncertainty. Even when people deliver, integrating what they produce into institutional ways of working can be difficult. For instance, citizens and their communities can educate. But how can their "lessons" fit into a standard curriculum? That will take extra effort and some ingenuity.

The Benefits

Even though the costs of doing business with the public are significant, so are the benefits. A *with* strategy reinforces what our institutions are trying to do but can't do alone. The coronavirus pandemic made that clear. The outpouring of citizen initiatives across the country was spectacular. Sadly, these bursts of civic energy tend to fall off sharply after the crisis passes, as happened after the 9/11 terrorist attack. Institutions benefit long term when working *with* people and it becomes more of a norm than an exception.

A CALL FOR INVENTORS

Does this report or the more detailed book it is based on have answers to questions about what a *with* strategy should look like in practice? No. These publications only offer a different way of thinking about the relationship between citizens and governing institutions. What the most useful applications can be will require imagination and innovation. And that will require experimentation, which is always risky. Inventors learn from failures, and both institutional authorities and citizens have to support them when they don't succeed. Despite the risks, experimentation is the only way to move forward when the best of conventional practices to combat the erosion of public confidence aren't working.

Democracy itself is an ongoing experiment. Democracy is also an ideal, and ideals are always being challenged by reality. There is no perfect example. It has been said that making democracy work as it should is a journey, not a destination. What keeps democracy alive are innovations that point to new possibilities. That is the real purpose of a *with* strategy, to encourage democratic inventiveness in both civic associations and governing institutions.

It is worth keeping in mind that democracy isn't just about elected or appointed officials in government. It is more than the clash of political parties in election contests. It is more than all of our institutions, nongovernmental as well as governmental, important as they are. Democracy is us—The People. And we can restore our sense of sovereignty in the same way Samuel Cooper's generation did, by what we produce every day using the abilities and resources of our fellow citizens. And when the things that happen frustrate, disappoint, and anger us—as they will—the question we have to ask ourselves is not what is wrong with democracy, but what are we going to do about it? That question can only be answered *with* one another.

ENDNOTES

[1] Brad Rourke, memorandum to Kettering Foundation deliberative politics, NIF issue guide, and institutional research workgroups, "A View from Rural America," March 30, 2018.

[2] Pew Research Center, "The Partisan Divide on Political Values Grows Even Wider," October 5, 2017, http://www.people-press.org/2017/10/05/the-partisan-divide-on-political-values-grows-even-wider/ (accessed May 29, 2018). Americans also believe that people's distrust of one another makes it more difficult to solve the country's problems. Pew Research Center, "Trust and Distrust in America," July 22, 2019, https://www.people-press.org/2019/07/22/trust-and-distrust-in-america/ (accessed January 17, 2020).

[3] Ian Anson, "Americans Distrusted US Democracy Long Before Trump's Russia Problem," The Conversation, http://theconversation.com/americans-distrusted-us-democracy-long-before-trumps-russia-problem-100082 (accessed July 18, 2018).

[4] Robert Teeter, "The Present National Political Attitude as Determined by Pre-Election Polls," November 1976, Box 62, Folder "Post-Election Analysis—Speeches and Reports (2)," Robert Teeter Papers, Gerald R. Ford Presidential Library, Ann Arbor, MI. One of the studies we have found useful in tracing declining confidence in government is Seymour Martin Lipset and William Schneider, *The Confidence Gap: Business, Labor, and Government in the Public Mind* (New York: The Free Press, 1983).

[5] Pew Research Center, *Beyond Distrust: How Americans View Their Government* (Pew Research Center, November 2015), 18.

[6] Laurie Kellman and Emily Swanson, "AP-NORC Poll: Three-Quarters in US Say They Lack Influence," Associated Press, July 12, 2017, https://www.apnews.com/a3eac6255194410eb2ab2166f09cd429/AP-NORC-Poll:-Three-quarters-in-US-say-they-lack-influence (accessed September 14, 2017).

[7] The Harwood Group, *Citizens and Politics: A View from Main Street America* (Dayton, OH: Kettering Foundation, 1991), 19.

[8] Seyla Benhabib et al., *The Democratic Disconnect: Citizenship and Accountability in the Transatlantic Community* (Washington, DC: Transatlantic Academy, 2013), vii. "What's Gone Wrong with Democracy," *Economist,* March 1, 2014, http://www.economist.com/news/essays/21596796-democracy-was-most-successful-political-idea-20th-century-why-has-it-run-trouble-and-what-can-be-do (accessed June 23, 2017).

[9] There is a survey of the negative perceptions that Washington officials have of citizens in Jennifer Bachner and Benjamin Ginsberg, *What Washington Gets Wrong* (Amherst, NY: Prometheus Books, 2016), 9-10, 15-18.

[10] In Latin, "*bellum omnium contra omnes.*" Thomas Hobbes, *Leviathan*, ed. C. B. Macpherson (New York: Penguin Books, 1968), 185.

[11] Abraham Lincoln speaking to the Illinois Republican State Convention, Springfield, IL, June 16, 1858.

[12] Jeffrey M. Jones, "Record-High 77% of Americans Perceive Nation as Divided," Gallup, November 21, 2016, https://news.gallup.com/poll/197828/record-high-americans-perceive-nation-divided.aspx (accessed March 6, 2018). Rick Hampson, "As Trump Hits 100 Days, Americans Agree: We're Still Divided," *USA Today*, April 28, 2017. Natalie Jackson and Ariel Edwards-Levy, "Huffpollster: The One Thing Americans Can Agree On Is That They're Divided," *Huffington Post*, November 29, 2016, https://www.huffingtonpost.com/entry/americans-agree-divided_us_583d8036e4b04b66c01ba9af (accessed March 6, 2018). John Wagner and Scott Clement, "'It's Just Messed Up': Most Think Political Divisions as Bad as Vietnam Era, New Poll Shows," *Washington Post*, October 28, 2017, https://www.washingtonpost.com/graphics/2017/national/democracy-poll/?utm_term=.d5c34dde0090 (accessed March 6, 2018).

[13] "USA TODAY NETWORK and Public Agenda to Explore the 'Hidden Common Ground' Among Citizens Leading to the 2020 Election," USA Today Network Pressroom, November 11, 2019, https://www.usatoday.com/ story/news/pr/2019/11/11/multi-platform-partnership-include-local-community-forums-sponsored-national-issues-forums-institute/2561645001/ (accessed January 28, 2020).

[14] Richard Wike et al., *Globally, Broad Support for Representative and Direct Democracy* (Pew Research Center, October 2017), and Roberto Stefan Foa and Yascha Mounk, "The Democratic Disconnect," *Journal of Democracy* 27, no. 3 (July 2016): 5-17.

[15] Adiel Suarez-Murias, *Civic Language Perceptions Project* (Philanthropy for Active Civic Engagement, 2019), http://www.pacefunders.org/wp-content/uploads/2019/05/PACE-Language-Perception-Project_May-16.pdf (accessed October 4, 2019).

[16] Brian J. Cook, *Bureaucracy and Self-Government: Reconsidering the Role of Public Administration in American Politics* (Baltimore, MD: Johns Hopkins University Press, 1996), 134-135.

[17] The foundation has been reading the literature in paleo-political anthropology for many years (reviews on file) as well as examining the work of scholars who found what we know of prehistoric times useful in understanding the earliest forms of politics. See Francis Fukuyama, *The Origins of Political Order: From Prehuman Times to the French Revolution* (New York: Farrar, Straus, and Giroux, 2011).

[18] See Robert Beekes, *Etymological Dictionary of Greek*, vol. 1 (Boston: Leiden, 2010), 325, 772; and Henry Liddell and Robert Scott, eds., *A Greek-English Lexicon* (Oxford: Clarendon Press, 1968), 386-387, 992.

[19] David Mathews, *The Ecology of Democracy: Finding Ways to Have a Stronger Hand in Shaping Our Future* (Dayton, OH: Kettering Foundation Press, 2014).

[20] Paul Arnsberger et al., "A History of the Tax-Exempt Sector: An SOI Perspective," *Statistics of Income Bulletin* (Winter 2008): 106, 124.

[21] Monica Schoch-Spana et al., "Community Engagement: Leadership Tool for Catastrophic Health Events," *Biosecurity and Bioterrorism: Biodefense Strategy, Practice, and Science* 5, no. 1 (2007): 10-11.

[22] Elinor Ostrom, "Covenanting, Co-Producing, and the Good Society," *PEGS* (Committee on the Political Economy of the Good Society) *Newsletter* 3, no. 2 (Summer 1993): 8.

[23] Ostrom, "Covenanting, Co-Producing, and the Good Society," 8.

[24] Global Agenda Council on the Future of Government, *Government with the People: A New Formula for Creating Public Value* (Cologny, Switzerland: World Economic Forum, February 2017).

[25] Samuel Cooper, *A Sermon Preached before His Excellency John Hancock, Esq., Governour, the Honourable the Senate, and House of Representatives of the Commonwealth of Massachusetts, October 25, 1780: Being the Day of the Commencement of the Constitution, and Inauguration of the New Government* (Boston: T. and J. Fleet, and J. Gill, 1780). See also Charles W. Akers, "Religion and the American Revolution: Samuel Cooper and the Brattle Street Church," *William and Mary Quarterly* 35, no. 3 (1978): 477-498.

[26] Bonnie Braun et al., *Engaging Unheard Voices: Under What Conditions Can, and Will, Limited Resource Citizens Engage in the Deliberative Public Policy Process?* (College Park, MD: Report to the Kettering Foundation, March 2006), 5.

[27] In the "Funeral Oration of Pericles," Pericles describes public deliberation as *prodidacthenai . . . logo*, or the talk Athenians use to teach themselves before they act. See Thucydides, *History of the Peloponnesian War* 2.40.2.

[28] Daniel Yankelovich, *Coming to Public Judgment: Making Democracy Work in a Complex World* (Syracuse, NY: Syracuse University Press, 1991), 95-96.

[29] Hannah Arendt, *Between Past and Future: Eight Exercises in Political Thought* (New York: Penguin Books, 1977), 220–221.

[30] James Fallows and Deborah Fallows, *Our Towns: A 100,000-Mile Journey into the Heart of America* (New York: Pantheon Books, 2018); James Fallows, "How America Is Putting Itself Back Together," *Atlantic* (March 2016), https://www.

theatlantic.com/magazine/archive/2016/03/how-america-is-putting-itself-back-together/426882/ (accessed October 19, 2018).

[31] Fallows, "How America Is Putting Itself Back Together."

[32] A classic study that demonstrates the health benefits of strong social networks was done in Roseto, Pennsylvania. There are several sources. I suggest John G. Bruhn and Stewart Wolf, *The Roseto Story: An Anatomy of Health* (Norman, OK: University of Oklahoma Press, 1979). Also see Marc Pilisuk and Susan Hillier Parks, *The Healing Web: Social Networks and Human Survival* (Hanover, NH: University Press of New England, 1986).

[33] Bobby Milstein, *Hygeia's Constellation: Navigating Health Futures in a Dynamic and Democratic World* (Atlanta, GA: Centers for Disease Control and Prevention, April 15, 2008), 54-57.

[34] "The relationship between social and community ties and mortality was assessed using . . . a random sample of 6,928 adults in Alameda County, California, and a subsequent nine-year mortality follow-up. The findings show that people who lacked social and community ties were more likely to die in the follow-up period than those with more extensive contacts." Lisa F. Berkman and S. Leonard Syme, "Social Networks, Host Resistance, and Mortality: A Nine-Year Follow-Up Study of Alameda County Residents," *American Journal of Epidemiology*, Vol. 109, Issue 2 (1979): 186-204.

[35] Francis Fukuyama, *Trust: The Social Virtues and the Creation of Prosperity* (New York: Free Press Paperbacks, 1995).

[36] John McKnight, "Associations and Their Democratic Functions" (Dayton, OH: Report to the Kettering Foundation), available at https://resources.depaul.edu/abcd-institute/publications/publications-by-topic/Documents/   Associations%20and%20Their%20Democratic%20Functions.pdf (accessed April 27, 2020).

[37] Patrick Sharkey, *Uneasy Peace: The Great Crime Decline, the Renewal of City Life, and the Next War on Violence* (New York: W. W. Norton, 2018).

[38] Emily Badger, "The Unsung Role That Ordinary Citizens Played in the Great Crime Decline," The Upshot, *New York Times*, November 9, 2017, https://nyti.ms/2hlT3Mu (accessed May 22, 2018).

[39] Badger, "The Unsung Role That Ordinary Citizens Played in the Great Crime Decline."

[40] Christopher Seddon, *Humans: From the Beginning* (Glanville Publications, 2015), 336-337, 345.

[41] James C. Scott, *Seeing Like a State: How Certain Schemes to Improve the Human Condition Have Failed* (New Haven, CT: Yale University Press, 1998).

⁴² Martha Derthick, *The Influence of Federal Grants: Public Assistance in Massachusetts* (Cambridge, MA: Harvard University Press, 1970), 79, 158-159.

⁴³ Philip K. Howard, *The Death of Common Sense: How Law Is Suffocating America* (New York: Random House, 1994).

⁴⁴ Delores Foley, "Sustaining Space and Developing Leadership for Public Deliberation Workshop: History and Impact of the Deliberative Dialogues Project at the University of Hawaii at Manoa," (Dayton, OH: Report to the Kettering Foundation, July 11, 2006).